SCIENCE

FORCES AND MOVEMENT

Claire Llewellyn

Evans

Published by Evans Brothers Limited
2A Portman Mansions
Chiltern Street
London W1U 6NR

© Evans Brothers Limited 2004
Reprinted 2005
Produced for Evans Brothers Limited by
White-Thomson Publishing Ltd.
2/3 St Andrew's Place
Lewes, East Sussex BN7 1UP

Printed in China by WKT Company Limited

Editor: Dereen Taylor
Consultants: Les Jones, Science Consultant, Manchester
Education Partnership; Norah Granger, former primary
headteacher and senior lecturer in education, University
of Brighton
Designer: Leishman Design

Cover: All photographs by Chris Fairclough

British Library Cataloguing in Publication Data
Llewellyn, Claire
    Forces and Movement - (Start-up science)
    1.Force and energy - Juvenile literature 2.Motion -
    Juvenile literature
    I.Title
    531.1

ISBN: 0 237 52587 9

Acknowledgements:
Special thanks to the following for their help and
involvement in the preparation of this book: Staff and
pupils at Elm Grove Primary School, Brighton, Liz
Price and family and friends, Christine Clark and family.

Picture Acknowledgements:
Chris Fairclough Colour Library 14; Ecoscene 6, 7 (top);
Popperfoto 7 (bottom), 15 (bottom right); WTPix 10.
All other photographs by Chris Fairclough.

Contents

Move that body!

We can move our body in all sorts of different ways.

▼ We can stretch our arms.

▲ We can swing one leg and then the other.

move   body

▼ We can bend at the hips and touch our toes.

▲ We can lift one leg and balance like a dancer.

How many different parts of your body can you move?
How many different ways can you move your arms?

stretch swing bend balance

How does it move?

Things move in many different ways. We use all sorts of words to describe them.

▶ Look at this picture of a snake. These words describe how a snake moves.

Can you think of another animal that moves like this?

slither

stretch

slide

glide

wriggle

slide   slither   glide   wriggle

How do cats and birds move?

Which of these words would you use to describe them?

Can you move like one of these animals?

soar stalk

flap fly jump leap

creep swoop

flutter

glide walk run pounce

flap   swoop   creep   flutter   pounce   7

On the move

Alex is getting on his scooter to find his friends in the park.

▼ When he **pushes** his foot against the ground, the wheels **turn** round, and the scooter **starts** to move.

▲ Alex wants to go **faster**. He pushes his foot down **harder** and faster. He is moving **quickly** now.

pushes turn starts faster harder

▼ Alex wants to turn **right** now. What does he have to do?

► Alex has found his friends. How did he **slow** down and **stop**?

quickly   right   slow   stop

Let's pull!

Pulling is a way of moving things. We pull on a hat when we put it on.

▼ This water skier is being pulled along by a boat.

A pull is a kind of force. It makes things happen.

pulling force

◀ Many things in this kitchen can be pulled. How many can you spot?

What would happen if you gave this plug and these apples a pull?

Let's push!

Pushing is a way of moving things. We **push** open a door.

► We push cymbals together to make them **CLASH!**

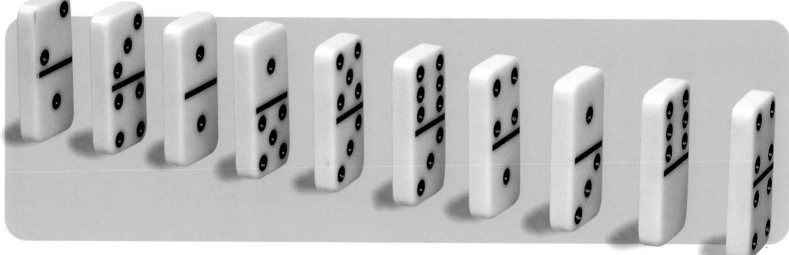

▲ A push is another kind of force. It makes things happen. Look at the dominoes in this picture. What would happen if you pushed the first one?

12

push   clash   wind

Wind **and** running water **can push things. They are forces, too.**

▲ **What is the force pushing this washing?**

► **What happens when Patrick puts his** water wheel **under the running water?**

running water   water wheel   13

In the playground

▶ Hanif is swinging high on the swing.
It goes forward and back.

▼ Archie and his friends are on the roundabout. It's spinning round and round.

How could Archie make it stop?

▼ Robbie and Nita are on the see-saw. It goes up and down.

How are they making the see-saw move?

forward   back   round

How do the things in these pictures move?

up   down

Rolling along

Becky and Ruth are playing skittles.

Becky rolls the ball along the ground. But she pushes the ball too gently… it does not knock the skittles down.

▶ Ruth pushes the ball much harder. The greater force makes the ball roll further. It knocks the skittles down.

rolls   gently   greater

▶ **Morrissey rolls a marble on a carpet, on grass, on concrete, and on sand. He tries to use the same force each time. He measures how far the marble goes and writes the results on a chart. Where does the marble roll best?**

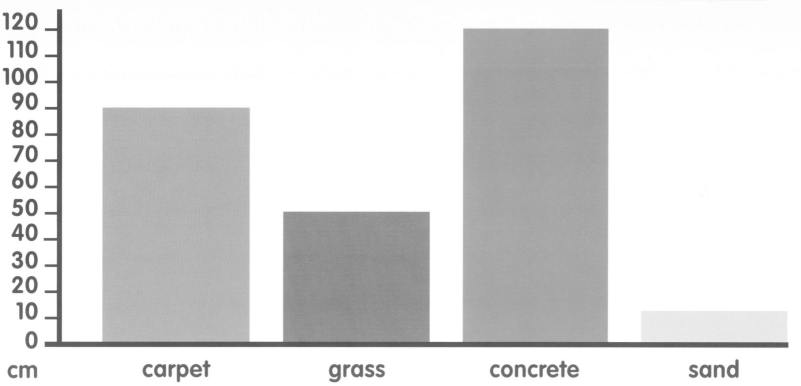

| cm | carpet | grass | concrete | sand |

Make it stop

Tom's little sister is playing with her buggy.

The buggy rolls away.

▼ Tom pulls it back to stop it.

A force can slow things down. It can make them stop.

It is safe to stop things if they are light. It can be dangerous if they are heavy.

Which one of these two objects would you be able to stop if it were racing towards you?

Which one is too heavy?

What would happen if you tried to stop it?

safe   light   dangerous   heavy

Changing shape

Josh is making a snail out of play dough. He pulls and pushes the dough to change its shape.

◀ First, he makes a thin strip,

▶ Then he curls it to make the shell.

change   shape   curls

▼ He pulls off some different-coloured dough to make the body. How does he make the horns?

▲ Latha is making a long, wriggly worm. Her worm might break in two. Do you know why?

break

Further information for

New words listed in the text:

back	curls	further	move	running water	swing
balance	dangerous	gently	pounce	safe	swoop
bend	down	glide	push	shape	turn
body	faster	greater	pushes	slide	up
break	flap	harder	pulling	slither	water wheel
change	flutter	heavy	quickly	slow	wind
clash	force	light	right	starts	wriggle
creep	forward	measures	rolls	stop	
			round	stretch	

Possible Activities

PAGES 4-5

Ask the children to write a sequence of three or four different movements, then choose someone in the class to perform them.

Take the children to watch people playing in the park or an adventure playground. How many different kinds of movement can they spot?

PAGES 6-7

Collect pictures of animals in movement. Ask children to suggest words that describe the way the animals move.

Write the names of different animals on pieces of card. Ask children to take a card and, without naming the animal, imitate the way it moves. Can other children guess what the animal is?

PAGES 8-9

Stand at the school gate and watch passing traffic start up, speed up, turn, slow down and stop.

Play with toy cars on a road mat. Ask children how they can make their car start moving, speed up, turn, slow down and stop.

PAGES 10-11

Ask children to choose an object in the classroom that they think can be moved by pulling. Now ask them to prove this.

Label all the things in the classroom that can be moved by pulling.

PAGES 12-13

Label all the things in the classroom that can be moved by pushing. Make a collection of toys and ask children how they can start each one moving. Now ask them to test their idea. Were they right?

Go outside on a breezy day and ask children to name all the things they can see moving in the wind.

Parents and Teachers

Blow bubbles with a soap and wand kit. Ask how the bubbles are formed.

PAGES 14-15

Make a list of things in the classroom that move forward and back, up and down, and round and round.

Many playgrounds have a slide. What can children do to slide down very fast? What can they do to slide down slowly?

PAGES 16-17

Hold races in which two or more children push toy cars along the ground. Measure the distances and make a table to record the results. Whose car goes the furthest of all? Discuss why.

Collect together balls of different weights and sizes. Ask children to choose a ball to knock down some skittles. Which one do they think will work the best? Now ask them to test their ideas and record the results.

PAGES 18-19

Take a trolley or pushchair into the classroom and ask children to demonstrate how they would safely stop it moving.

Discuss why roads are dangerous. Look at a video or CD-Rom about road safety.

PAGES 20-21

Make animals with Plasticine or clay. Ask children to describe each action they use to shape the material. Is it a push or a pull?

Further Information

BOOKS FOR CHILDREN

How? What? Why?: What makes it swing? by J Pipe (Franklin Watts, 2002)

Little Bees: And Everyone Shouted 'Pull!' by Claire Llewellyn (Hodder Wayland, 2002)

The Seesaw and Other Science Questions by Brenda and Stuart Naylor (Hodder Wayland, 2000)

Ways into Science: Push and Pull by Peter Riley (Franklin Watts, 2001)

WEBSITES

www.educate.org.uk
www.howstuffworks.com
www.local-transport.dft.gov.uk/schooltravel/safe
www.primaryresources.co.uk/science

Index